中 国 长 城
THE GREAT WALL OF CHINA

登 长 城 纪 念
MEMORY OF CLIMBING THE GREAT WALL

此证颁发给

This is to certify that _____

攀登长城日期、地点

Did climb the Great Wall on _____

長城

THE GREAT WALL

DIE GROSSE MAUER
LA GRANDE MURAILLE

京华出版社

长城是中国古代一项伟大的防御工程。它从东到西绵延一万余华里，宛如一条巨龙，穿沙漠、过草原、越群山、蜿蜒起伏于中国北方辽阔的山川大地上，堪称人类建筑史上的奇迹，1987年被联合国教科文组织列入了世界文化遗产名录。

公元前7世纪前后，是中国历史上春秋战国时代。由于各诸侯国之间为了相互防御，各自修筑了防御邻国的长城。公元前221年，秦始皇统一了中国，为了国家的统一，防御北方的游牧民族对中原地区的骚扰，下令拆毁了内部原各国的长城、关隘，沿用部分北面、东面的旧长城，修筑了西起临洮，东至辽东，全长一万多华里的长城，始称万里长城。秦代（公元前221年—公元前206年）以后，许多朝代都对长城有过修筑，其中汉代（公元前206年—公元220年）长城较之秦代更有所发展，并修筑了外长城，使之长度达到了两万余华里。明代（公元1368年—公元1644年）是修筑长城的最后一个朝代，明代长城工程之浩大，自秦汉之后，没有哪一个朝代能够与之相比。工程技术也达到了一个新的高度，建筑结构更加坚固、合理，防御的作用也更加显著。我们现在所看到的长城，大部分为明代所修筑。它东起山海关，西到嘉峪关，横跨中国北方七个省、市、自治区，长度约6000余公里。明代建都北京，所以北京周边的长城修建得更为险奇、坚固，也最为壮观。

长城的主体为绵延万里的高大城墙，把成千上万座城台、敌楼、隘口、城关、烽火台等连缀为一体。城墙随山形地势而筑，千变万化，城墙均高约7—8米，宽约5米，可容五马并骑。城上建有宇墙，墙上开有垛口，用于瞭望，下部有射洞，用于攻击敌人。城墙上每隔一段即有一个骑墙的台子，低的叫城台，是士卒巡逻放哨的地方，有的城台建有铺房，为遮风避雨之用。高的叫敌楼，有两层、三层的，用于守望和住宿并储存武器、弹药，以打击来犯之敌。城墙内外还建有许多独立的高台子，称为烽火台，白天燃烟、夜间放火来传递军情。关塞隘口是平时出入长城的要道，也是重点防守的据点。城堡障堠分布在长城内外，用以驻兵防守。

长城是中华民族最伟大的创造，是中华民族勤劳智慧的象征。中国有句名言："不到长城非好汉。"希望世界上热爱旅游的朋友们都有机会到中国，亲眼看一看这一人类历史上的奇迹——长城。

The Great Wall was a great defence project of ancient China. Stretching more than 10,000 li (5,000 kilometres), it extends through deserts, grasslands and mountains from eastern to western parts of North China. This wonder in the human architectural history was listed as a world cultural heritage by the United Nations Educational, Scientific and Cultural Organization in 1987.

The Great Wall was built around the Seventh Century BC, which was the Spring and Autumn and Warring States period in the Chinese history. States built their walls to guard against each other. In 221 BC, Emperor Qinshihuang united the whole country. To maintain the national unity and prevent the northern nomadic tribes from harassing the central plains area, he had the 5,000-kilometre wall built, which started from Lintao in the west and ended in eastern Liaoning. The 10,000-li Great Wall got its name since then. The construction of the Great Wall stopped in the Ming Dynasty (1368-1644) when China's engineering technology had also reached a new height. The Great Wall was more solid and better designed for the purpose of defence. The Great Wall we see now was mostly built in that dynasty. More than 6,000 kilometers long, it began from Shanhaiguan and ended in Jiayuguan, running through China's seven northern provinces, autonomous regions and municipalities. As Beijing was the capital during the Ming Dynasty, the Great Wall near Beijing looks more solid, precipitous and magnificent.

The mainbody of the Great Wall was the tall wall that stretches 5,000 kilometres and links thousands of terraces, battle forts, mountain passes, and beacon towers. The wall rises and falls with the mountains. Seven to eight metres tall and five metres wide, it can accommodate five horses going side by side. Concave wall was built for soldiers to watch enemies. In the middle of the wall were shooting holes. There were platforms between every section of the wall. The lower platforms were called bench-tables, where soldiers stood sentry. Some platforms with rooms built, were used as shealters sentry. Some platforms with rooms built, were used as shealters against the wind and the rain. The higher platforms (with two or three storeys) were called battle forts. They were used as places for observation and lodging as well as storing weapons and ammunitions against the invaders. Many separate high terraces were also built inside and outside the wall. They were called beacon towers. During the daytime, smoke was lit and at night, fire was set to pass on information. The passes were the most important paths to enter and get out of the Great Wall and fortresses for defence. The defence castles, distributed inside and outside the Great Wall, were stationed by soldiers.

The Great Wall is the greatest creation and the symbol of the wisdom and diligence of the Chinese nation. There is an old saying in China: "One can be called a true man only after he has reached the Great Wall." It is our hope that friends who love tourism all over the world will have an opportunity to come to China and see the Great Wall——a wonder in human history.

長城は中国古代の偉大な防御工程である。東から西へ1万里（1里＝0.5キロメートル）以上長く伸びていて、巨大な龍のように、砂漠を通り抜け、草原を通り過ぎ、群山を登り越し、中国北方の広い国土にえんえんと曲がりくねって続いて、人類建築史上の奇跡と言われ、1987年に国連教育科学文化機構に世界文化遺産名簿に取り入れた。

紀元前7世紀前後は中国歴史の春秋戦国時代である。各諸侯国の間に相互防御のために、それぞれ隣国防御用の長城を構築した。紀元前221年、始皇帝は中国を統一した。国の統一と北方遊牧民族による中原地域への侵犯を防御するため、命令を出して中国国内の元各国の長城や関所を取壊し、一部の北側と東側の旧長城を利用して西の臨　から東の遼東までの1万里の長城を構築した。これは万里長城と言った。秦の時代（紀元前221年～紀元前206年）以後、多くの時代には長城を修築し、その内、漢の時代（紀元前206年～紀元220年）は秦より長城がもっと伸びて、外長城も修築し、長さが2万里以上となった。明の時代（紀元1368年～紀元1644年）は長城修築の最後の王朝で、明の時代に長城工程の規模が秦、漢以後、比べるものにならないほど極めて大きい。工程の技術も新しい高度に達し、建築構造が一層堅くて合理的で、防御の役割ももっと顕著になった。現在人々が見る長城の大部分は明の時代に修築したものである。東には山海関から始め、西には嘉峪関まで、中国北方の七つの省、市、自治区を跨り、長さがおよそ6000キロメートル以上である。明の首都は北京であるので、北京周辺の長城は一層険しくて堅く、最も壮観である。

長城の主体は長く伸びている高い城壁であり、数えられない城台、望楼、関所、烽火台等を一体に接続する。城壁は山の地形地勢に沿って修築し、変化きわまりなく、高さが約7～8メートルで、幅が約5メートルで、5匹の馬が並列で走ることができる。城の上に宇壁が建てられ、壁に穴を開けて敵情を監視し、下部には矢を射る穴を設けて敵を攻撃する。城壁に一定の距離おきに台があり、低い台は壁台と言い、兵士が巡邏歩哨をおくのところ、ある台に寝台付ける部屋を立てて兵士が巡邏する時に風雨の遮蔽に使う。高い台は望楼と言い、2階や3階のものがあって、敵情の監視や宿泊、敵を打撃するための武器、弾薬の貯蔵に使う。城壁の内外には多くの独立の高台を構築し、烽火台と言い、昼には煙を出して、夜には火を燃えて軍事情報を伝達するのである。関所は常時長城の出入り要路で、重点的に防衛の拠点でもある。牙城や垣などは長城の内外に分布され、駐屯兵に使う。

長城は中華民族の最も偉大な創造であり、中華民族の勤勉と智慧のシンボルである。中国の有名なことわざ：「長城に行かないと堂々たる男子でない。」世界で旅行が好きな友達がチャンスを作って中国に来て自らこの人類歴史の奇跡——長城をぜひ見て頂きたいと思う。

La Grande Muraille est un traveaux colossale de défense de la Chine antique, elle s'étendent de l'est à l'ouest comme un drogon géant sur une longueur de 10000 li. Elle traverse le désert, la steppe, et monte sur des chaînes de montagnes, ondule en zigzagant sur une vaste étendue de plaine du Nord de la Chine. La Grande Muraille est digne d'être considérée comme un miracle dans l'histoire de l'architecture de l'humanité, elle a été inclue en 1987 par l'UNESCO dans le registre de l'héritage de la culture mondiale.

Sept siècles environ avant notre ère, c'était l'époque des Printemps et des Automnes et des Royaumes Combattants dans l'histoire de la Chine. Les différentes principautés des vassaux ont construit chacune leur propore muraille pour se défendre contre leurs voisins ennemis. L'année 221 avant notre ère, le Shihuang des Qins, après avoir unifié la Chine toute entière, a fait construire la Grande Muraille allant de Lintao de l'ouest à Liaodong de l'est sur une longeur de 10000 li en vue de la réunification de la Chine et de la défense contre le harcèlement des ethnies nomades du Nord dans les plaines de la partie centrale du pays. C'était à partir de ce moment là que l'on commençait à la nommer "la Grande Muraille de 10000 li" . La Dynastie des Ming (1368—1644) est la dernière dynastie où l'on poursuivait encore la construction de la Muraille. A cette époque, le niveau de la technologie des traveaux a atteint à un nouveau degré, la structure architecturale était plus que jamais solide et rationnelle, et le rôle de défense de la Muraille était encore plus évident. La grande Muraille que nous voyons aujourd'hui fut construite pour la plupart de ses traveaux à la Dynastie des Ming. Elle va à l'est de la Passe Shanhaiguang jusqu'à la Passe de Jiayuguang à l'ouest en traversant 7 provinces, villes et régions autonomes des minorité nationales avec une longeur de 6000 KM environ.Etant donné que la Dynastie des Ming a établi la capitale à Beijing, c'est pourquoi les tronçons de la Muraille à la périphérie de Beijing sont plus escarpés, plus solides et plus imposants qu'ailleur.

Le gros de la Grande Muraille est la muraille colossale qui relie en un ensemble des dizaines des miliers de tours de guet, de créneaux, de cols, de tours du feu d'alarme. La muraille fut construite selon la topographie du terrain en zigzag. En général, la muraille est haute de 7 à 8 mètres, large de 5 mètres sur laquelle peuvent passer en même temps 5 chevaux. Sur la muraille, il y a des ramparts au milieu desquels sont creusés des créneaux d' observation,et en bas de ces créneaux, il y a des trous par lesquels on attaque les ennemis avec arc et flèche. A l'intérieur comme à l'extérieur de la Muraille, se dressent encore des tours plus ou moins isolées appelées "tours du feu d'alarme" . S'il a quelque situation ennemie à signaler, il doit y avoir de la fumée pendant la journée et du feu durant la nuit. Les passes et les cols sont accès principaux de la Muraille, ils sont aussi des points clés à défendre. Les châteaux forts parsemés à l'intérieur comme à l'extérieur de la Muraille étaient les lieux de garnisons des troupes.

La grande Muraille est la plus grande création de la Nation chinoise, elle est aussi le symbole de la diligence et de la sagesse de notre nation. Un proverbe chinois dit:"Celui qui n'a jamais grempé sur la Grande Muraille n'est pas un brave homme" . Nous espérons que tous les amis des pays du monde passionnés pour le tourisme auront l'occasion de voyger en Chine et de voir de leurs propres yeux la Grande Muraille —— une des merveilles dans l'histoire de l'humanité.

Die Grosse Mauer, eine grossartige Verteidigungsanlage in alten Zeiten Chinas, erstreckt sich vom Osten nach Westen ueber eine Laenge von zehn tausend Li(entspricht fuenf tausend Km) wie einen riesigen Drachen, der durch die Wuesten laeuft , die Steppen ueberquert und ueber die Bergketten wandert. Auf und nieder schlaengelt sich die Grosse Mauer ueber die weitraeumigen Gebirge und Fluesse im Nordchina. Sie kann als ein Wunder der Baugeschichte der Menschheit betrachtet werden und in 1987 wurde sie durch UNESCO auf die Liste des kulturellen Welterbe gesetzt.

Ungefaehr im 7. Jahrhundert v.u.Z(vor unserer Zeitrechnung) ist es in Fruehlings-und Herbst Periode sowie streitender Periode in der chinesischen Geschichte. Zur gegenseitigen Verteidigung der Aggression der anderen Lehnsfuerstenslaendern wurden die Grossen Mauern von jeweiligen Laendern aufgebaut. In 221 v.u.Z(vor unserer Zeitrechnung) vereinigte Qinshihuang(der erste Kaiser von Qin-Dynastie) alle Lehnsfuerstenslaender in China. Um einen geeinten Staat zu errichten, um vor der Stoer-und Sabotagetaetigkeit des Nomadenvolks im Nordchina auf den zentralen Gebiete Chinas(am Mittel-und Unterlauf des Huanghe-Flusses) zu schuetzen, wurde die Grosse Mauer mit einer Gesamtlaenge von ueber zehn tausend Li (gleich fuenf tausend Kilometer) aufgebaut, die im Westen vom Lintao bis zum Liaodong im Osten lief, und von da an als Grosse Mauer von zehn tausend Li genannt wurde. Die Ming-Dynastie(von 1368n.u.Z. bis zum 1644 n.u.Z.) ist die letzte Dynastie, in welcher die Grosse Mauer wiedergebaut wurde. Die Bautechnik in der Ming-Dynastie hat sie schon ein neues Niveau erreicht. Der konstruktive Aufbau der Grossen Mauer ist noch staerker und rationeller, und die Grosse Mauer bietet eine noch sichtbarereVerteidigungswirkung an. Die Grosse Mauer, die wir heute sehen, ist groesstenteils in der Ming-Dynastie gebaut. Sie entspringt oestlich in Shanhaiguan-Pass und kommt westlich in Jiayuguan-Pass

zum Ende. Mit einer Laenge von ca. 6,000 km spannt sich die Grosse Mauer ueber sieben Provinzen, Staedte und autonome Gebiete im Nordchina. Weil die Ming-Dynastie ihre Hauptstadt in Beijing errichtet hatte, ist deswegen der Teil der Grossen Mauer, der um Beijing herum gebaut wurde, noch schroffer, staerker und auch am grossartigsten.

Der Hauptteil der Grossen Mauer besteht aus sich ueber zehn tausend Li erstreckenden hohen Stadtmauern, die tausend und aber tausend Stadttuerme, Wachtuerme, Gebirgspaesse, Gebiete unmittelbar vor dem Stadttor, Alarmfeuertuerme usw. zu einer vollstaendigen Einheit verbinden. Die Stadtmauern, die durchschnittlich ungefaehr 7 bis 8 Meter hoch und 5 Meter breit sind, sind nach den Gelaendeverhaeltnissen der Gebirge gebaut und sehen wechselvoll aus. Darauf koennen fuenf Pferde parall laufen. Auf den Stadtmauern kann man auch die Verteidigungsmauern sehen, worauf Zinnenluecken gemacht sind, damit man in die Ferne sehen kann. Unter den Zinnenluecken sind die Schiessscharten, die zum Schiessen der Feinde dienen. Zu beiden Seiten der Stadtmauer liegen noch viele alleinstehende Tuerme, die als Alarmfeuerturm genannt sind, wo man am Tag Rauch und in der Nacht Feuer produziert, damit die militaerischen Nachrichten weitergegeben werden koennen. Die Gebirgspaesse sind gewoehnlich die wichtige Verkehrsader der Grossen Mauer. Gleichzeitig sind sie auch Festungen, die schwerpunktmaessig zu verteidigen sind. Zu beiden Seiten der Grossen Mauer sind Burgen verteilt, wo die Verteidigungstruppe stationieren kann.

Die Grosse Mauer ist das groesste Erzeugnis und das Symbol der Tuechtigkeit sowie Weisheit der Chinesichen Nation. In China gibt es ein Sprichwort: " Wer die Grosse Mauer nicht erreicht, ist kein ganzer Kerl." Wir heissen alle Tourismus liebenden Freunde aus aller Welt in China willkommen, das Wunder der Menschheitsgeschichte——die Grosse Mauer mit eigenen Augen zu sehen.

长城之春
The Great Wall in spring
長城の春
Le printemps sur le Grande Muraille
Die Grosse Mauer im Frühling

长城之夏
The Great Wall in summer
長城の夏
Le Grande Muraille en été
Die Grosse Mauer im Sommer

长城之秋
The Great Wall in autumn
長城の秋
La Grande Muraille en automne
Die Grosse Mauer im Herbst

长城之冬
The Great Wall in winter
長城の冬
La Grande Muraille en hiver
Die Grosse Mauer im Winter

八达岭长城
The Great Wall at Badaling
八達嶺長城
La Grande Muraille à Badaling
Die Grosse Mauer bei Badaling

金山岭长城
The Great Wall at Jinshanling
金山嶺長城
La Grande Muraille à Jinshanling
Die Grosse Mauer bei Jinshanling

八达岭长城
The Great Wall at Badaling
八達嶺長城
La Grande Muraille à Badaling
Die Grosse Mauer bei Badaling

望京楼（司马台长城）
The Great Wall at Simatai
望京楼（司馬台長城）
La Grande Muraille à Simatai
Die Grosse Mauer bei Simatai

八达岭长城
The Great Wall at Badaling
八達嶺長城
La Grande Muraille à Badaling
Die Grosse Mauer bei Badaling

箭扣长城
The Great Wall at Jiankou
箭扣長城
La Grande Muraille à Jiankou
Die Grosse Mauer bei Jiankou

八达岭长城
The Great Wall at Badaling
八達嶺長城
La Grande Muraille à Badaling
Die Grosse Mauer bei Badaling

金山岭长城
The Great Wall at Jinshanling
金山嶺長城
La Grande Muraille à Jinshanling
Die Grosse Mauer bei Jinshanling

八达岭长城
The Great Wall at Badaling
八達嶺長城
La Grande Muraille à Badaling
Die Grosse Mauer bei Badaling

八达岭长城
The Great Wall at Badaling
八達嶺長城
La Grande Muraille à Badaling
Die Grosse Mauer bei Badaling

八达岭长城
The Great Wall at Badaling
八達嶺長城
La Grande Muraille à Badaling
Die Grosse Mauer bei Badaling

金山岭长城月色
Bright Moon over Jinshanling
金山岭長城日暮の月色
La pleine lune à la Jinshanling
Der helle Mond uber dem Jinshanling

八达岭长城
The Great Wall at Badaling
八達嶺長城
La Grande Muraille à Badaling
Die Grosse Mauer bei Badaling

八达岭长城
The Great Wall at Badaling
八達嶺長城
La Grande Muraille à Badaling
Die Grosse Mauer bei Badaling

金山岭长城
The Great Wall at Jinshanling
金山嶺長城
La Grande Muraille à Jinshanling
Die Grosse Mauer bei Jinshanling

金山岭长城
The Great Wall at Jinshanling
金山嶺長城
La Grande Muraille à Jinshanling
Die Grosse Mauer bei Jinshanling

仙女楼（司马台长城）
The Great Wall at Simatai
仙女楼（司馬台長城）
La Grande Muraille à Simatai
Die Grosse Mauer bei Simatai

八达岭长城
The Great Wall at Badaling
八達嶺長城
La Grande Muraille à Badaling
Die Grosse Mauer bei Badaling

望京楼（司马台长城）
Wangjinglou (The Great Wall at Simatai)
望京楼（司馬台長城）
Wangjinglou (La Grande Muraille à Simatai)
Wangjinglou (Die Grosse Mauer bei Simatai)

八达岭长城
The Great Wall at Badaling
八達嶺長城
La Grande Muraille à Badaling
Die Grosse Mauer bei Badaling

八达岭长城
The Great Wall at Badaling
八達嶺長城
La Grande Muraille à Badaling
Die Grosse Mauer bei Badaling

司马台长城

The Great Wall at Simatai

司馬台長城

La Grande Muraille à Simatai

Die Grosse Mauer bei Simatai

金山岭长城
The Great Wall at Jinshanling
金山嶺長城
La Grande Muraille à Jinshanling
Die Grosse Mauer bei Jinshanling

箭扣长城
The Great Wall at Jiankou
箭扣長城
La Grande Muraille à Jiankou
Die Grosse Mauer bei Jiankou

金山岭长城
The Great Wall at Jinshanling
金山嶺長城
La Grande Muraille à Jinshanling
Die Grosse Mauer bei Jinshanling

慕田峪长城正关台
Mutianyu Pass
慕田峪長城の正関台
La Passe Mutianyu
Die Pass Mutianyu

八达岭长城
The Great Wall at Badaling
八達嶺長城
La Grande Muraille à Badaling
Die Grosse Mauer bei Badaling

长城之冬
The Great Wall in winter
長城の冬
La Grande Muraille en hiver
Die Grosse Mauer im Winter

金山岭长城
The Great Wall at Jinshanling
金山嶺長城
La Grande Muraille à Jinshanling
Die Grosse Mauer bei Jinshanling

金山岭长城
The Great Wall at Jinshanling
金山嶺長城
La Grande Muraille à Jinshanling
Die Grosse Mauer bei Jinshanling

金山岭长城
The Great Wall at Jinshanling
金山嶺長城
La Grande Muraille à Jinshanling
Die Grosse Mauer bei Jinshanling

司马台长城
The Great Wall at Simatai
司馬台長城
La Grande Muraille à Simatai
Die Grosse Mauer bei Simatai

八达岭长城
The Great Wall at Badaling
八達嶺長城
La Grande Muraille à Badaling
Die Grosse Mauer bei Badaling

八达岭长城
The Great Wall at Badaling
八達嶺長城
La Grande Muraille à Badaling
Die Grosse Mauer bei Badaling

长城之春
The Great Wall in spring
長城の春
Le printemps sur le Grande Muraille
Die Grosse Mauer im Frühling

望京楼（司马台长城）
Wangjinglou (The Great Wall at Simatai)
望京楼（司馬台長城）
Wangjinglou (La Grande Muraille à Simatai)
Wangjinglou (Die Grosse Mauer bei Simatai)

慕田峪长城
The Great Wall at Mutianyu
慕田峪長城
La Grande Muraille à Mutianyu
Die Grosse Mauer bei Mutianyu

慕田峪长城
The Great Wall at Mutianyu
慕田峪長城
La Grande Muraille à Mutianyu
Die Grosse Mauer bei Mutianyu

雪后长城
The Great Wall wrapped in snow
白銀の装い
La Grande Muraille sous la neige
Ein schneebedeckter Abschnitt der Grossen

金山岭长城
The Great Wall at Jinshanling
金山嶺長城
La Grande Muraille à Jinshanling
Die Grosse Mauer bei Jinshanling

八达岭长城
The Great Wall at Badaling
八達嶺長城
La Grande Muraille à Badaling
Die Grosse Mauer bei Badaling

雪后长城
The Great Wall wrapped in snow
白銀の装い
La Grande Muraille sous la neige
Ein schneebedeckter Abschnitt der Grossen Mauer

八达岭长城
The Great Wall at Badaling
八達嶺長城
La Grande Muraille à Badaling
Die Grosse Mauer bei Badaling

慕田峪长城
The Great Wall at Mutianyu
慕田峪長城
La Grande Muraille à Mutianyu
Die Grosse Mauer bei Mutianyu

金山岭长城
The Great Wall at Jinshanling
金山嶺長城
La Grande Muraille à Jinshanling
Die Grosse Mauer bei Jinshanling

司马台长城
The Great Wall at Simatai
司馬台長城
La Grande Muraille à Simatai
Die Grosse Mauer bei Simatai

八达岭长城
The Great Wall at Badaling
八達嶺長城
La Grande Muraille à Badaling
Die Grosse Mauer bei Badaling

金山岭长城
The Great Wall at Jinshanling
金山嶺長城
La Grande Muraille à Jinshanling
Die Grosse Mauer bei Jinshanling

仙女楼（司马台长城）
The Great Wall at Simatai
仙女楼（司馬台長城）
La Grande Muraille à Simatai
Die Grosse Mauer bei Simatai

八达岭长城
The Great Wall at Badaling
八達嶺長城
La Grande Muraille à Badaling
Die Grosse Mauer bei Badaling

金山岭长城
The Great Wall at Jinshanling
金山嶺長城
La Grande Muraille à Jinshanling
Die Grosse Mauer bei Jinshanling

八达岭长城
The Great Wall at Badaling
八達嶺長城
La Grande Muraille à Badaling
Die Grosse Mauer bei Badaling

金山岭长城
The Great Wall at Jinshanling
金山嶺長城
La Grande Muraille à Jinshanling
Die Grosse Mauer bei Jinshanling

我 1964 年出生于长城脚下的妫川大地。1981 年 8 月到八达岭特区工作至今，现任八达岭长城报社职业摄影师。

多年来，我把到八达岭长城摄影的摄影师及摄影爱好者全部视为自己的老师，认真地向他们学习、请教。并且搜集所有有关长城的影集、图片等，从中吸取精华，不断地摸索经验，提高自己的摄影水平。

几年来，我拍摄了许多有关长城的图片，先后出版发行了多套长城明信片，并在许多报刊杂志上发表过关于长城的摄影作品。

这本《长城》摄影集的出版，是我多年的梦想。非常感谢八达岭特区党委和领导对我多年来的关心、帮助和支持，使我在摄影艺术上有了长足的发展，使《长城》摄影集得以顺利出版。我要像长城上的砖石一样，恪守在这古老的长城上，用手中的像机表现这一中国历史上最伟大的工程 —— 长城。

柳魁

2001 年 5 月，于八达岭长城

图文编辑：邢延生
责任编辑：孙志文
装帧设计：邢延生
电脑制作：褚　林

图书在版编目（CIP）数据

长城／柳魁摄. —北京：京华出版社，2001
ISBN 7-80600-592-7

Ⅰ.长…　Ⅱ.柳…　Ⅲ.长城—摄影集
Ⅳ.K928.71-64

中国版本图书馆 CIP 数据核字 (2001) 第 031091 号

长　城

著　者　柳魁
出版发行　京华出版社（北京市安华西里 1 区 13 楼　100011）
　　　　　　（010）64258473　64255036　64243832
印　刷　北京市佳信达艺术印刷有限公司
开　本　787×1092　1/12
印　张　6
印　数　3000
出版日期　2001 年 6 月第 1 版　2001 年 6 月第 1 次印刷
书　号　ISBN 7-80600-592-7/J · 27

京华版图书，若有质量问题，请与本社联系